EARNEST, EARNEST?

ELEANOR BOUDREAU

UNIVERSITY OF PITTSBURGH PRESS

Published by the University of Pittsburgh Press, Pittsburgh, Pa., 15260
Copyright © 2020, Eleanor Boudreau
All rights reserved
Manufactured in the United States of America
Printed on acid-free paper
10 9 8 7 6 5 4 3 2 1

ISBN 13: 978-0-8229-6630-2
ISBN 10: 0-8229-6630-1

Cover art: Early 1900s "Let's travel together" postcard, photographer
and production company unknown

Cover design: Alex Wolfe

EARNEST,

EARNEST?

PITT POETRY SERIES

ED OCHESTER, EDITOR

for Jeni McFarland, a fantastic friend and fiction writer,
I hope you enjoy this book of poetry

CONTENTS

EARNEST,

EARNEST?

The Heart Is Not a Synonym for the Chest

What you called a *cloud* was not a cloud. I am in hell here. Hell is a party where I don't sing and don't dance and someone turns to me and says, "You are a very pretty girl. Don't ever forget that."

I spend all night tramping up and down the staircase trying to figure out if you really love me.

Each stair a copy of the first and each of your words a copy of the one before it—*love, love, love*—above us an 18-wheeler on the highway bucks and shifts—*fishtailing*—and you think of me.

I would think of you, too, bucking and shifting, but that is not my heart.

That is my left breast.

There is a photocopier at the top of the staircase. I make a
photocopy of my heart for you. It says: WTF?!

I am in hell and I have picked up some of the language.

If I was Eurydice I would not not be mad at Orpheus—
I'd be the register above.

The truck, our house, our life together—these things I do not miss. A reminder written out on every mirror, "You are a very attractive lady—don't ever forget."

This I do not miss.

The bathroom with its three mirrors—I am happy, humming to myself in the morning, when you enter. You appear behind me again and lay your hand over my left hip, like a shadow.

This I do not miss.

The bathroom beginning to look like a lobster trap with its yellow bars of reflected light and my skin turning pink with sex again—

This

I miss—the knowledge that there is blood and it is pounding, fishy rivers beneath the skin, sperming toward an inland island.

"A long time ago, the Greeks poured out of their horse and stormed the city—

and there was nothing the Trojans could do."

I wanted to have you and be rid of you, Dear Earnest. Like a postcard
inside an envelope, I wanted it both ways, but I wasn't messing around.

All day long the children walked back and forth across the ice, the one we call Rachel
and the one we call Pickle. I walked across the ice as well, and I didn't break it.

Rachel held a lead rope, and Pickle pulled her sled-like through the driveway.
"I got snow down my pants," Rachel said. I wasn't messing around.

Back inside, Pickle shows me a piece of ice. "It is a scared piece of ice, Eleanor," she says.
There is a crack the shape of a 6 or a tadpole, I can see through the ice to her palm.

There is no delicate way to put this, Pick—
What happened to your gloves?

What else can I tell you? What else is true?
The child I did not have belonged to you.

9:32 p.m. ——

Our fists deep in the beef, we form lumps that, baked,
      swell with juices.
We used the knife to slice—first, mushrooms, then peaches.
Enough tenderness for one day has been kneaded
      and diced neatly. I remove
to wash the knife and lose my balance over the counter.
My hand flattens, fingers splayed against blade and basin.
      I cut myself. "What are you doing?"
I turn and look surprised, "My hand is . . . ," I start to say,
      flush with the sink.

One Thousand Words on Regret

Last night, I had sex for as long as it takes to drive to the gas station
  (on Cambridge St.)
and all the silver sperm capsized in the jelly, like beached fish—
  imagine their surprise.
                    Give me 1,000 words on regretfulness.

Sitting in the grass, I am trying to write out I hate you, "I have,
  I gave, I gate—"
                    and it's just too difficult to do. I gate you.

My jaw hurts and so I say it out loud, "My jaw hurts." And that just
  makes it hurt worse.
Swallow a candy in panic and it just sits in your stomach. Please,
  there is room—
                    make use of the furniture.

The title on your bookshelf *Whores on the Hillside* and I say,
  "Whales are mammals
and abortions don't take place in your stomach."
                                      A trailing,
smoky breath primed for the coming extinction. *I know that
  I'm not stupid.*
                    In their paddock the horses roar, like dinosaurs.

Bully for me! That's the creative spirit! The sunlight
  on the roof's stone banisters—
a missive reads, "Missing: a pair of tan/gold fishnets"—tights. Help!

The whole world is turning into words and I don't believe them.

The Plenum

For future generations I'll say this:
we were the first to speak with aliens.
We broadcast it. We said
the world is full and clean. The world is
full and clean.

———

I slide my sweatered arm across the table, so my fist is between us,
my fist and a little piece of naked wrist, a sick, unburied bulb,
but slide a clump of fingers out and my hand becomes
a gnarled root, white chap-lines like wiry hairs stuck tightly: ginger
and gingerly you take it and push the fingers out, they open terribly
like a flower and your fingers stroke my palm. *How long has it been
since you wrote a poem?*

———

It is not snowing but something keeps falling, falling, falling
outside the window. Just try to make it through the sun-soaked pasture,
    the light heavy
and lying on the pasture grass, so the grass is yellow-white with it and
    seething slightly,
a frying pan full of melted butter.
It is a gorgeous day and you always had a weakness for beauty,
could never keep your dick out of it. I would come home
and find the vases violated.

———

The light is soft, though, and nice,
like the teapot and its neighbor right now, the cozy.
They are nice, but this is not a nice restaurant—and thank God
we don't live in a nice restaurant—so I can talk about sex
and talk about sex the way I want to talk about sex, for example,

———

me explaining to no one (special, that is) that being a stud
is not always being a STUD—
these days it is all done by artificial insemination, plus
the way they extract the semen from you is not that fun.
I move my elbows as I do it—
behind my ribs, in front of my ribs, behind my ribs, in front of my ribs,
my forearms perpendicular, palms facing the ceiling.
That former racehorse with his soft wet eye . . . you see as he
emerges from the light and grazes, pastoral, a foot from our French windows,
but how often do you think of him?
You turn and blow me a kiss

———

and I think you mean it. Still.

10:13 a.m. —

I can't stop, I can't
stop looking at my watch.

Historically, We Haven't Taken Any Prisoners

Carpet is like heaven, where the angels rest and play,
until it burns, but
                    already the voice in my head is saying,
Okay, now agree with whatever he says.
                              If I've been warned once,
then I've been warned. You see the toothy shadow of a fence.
I see the threat
              of nightfall on the grass, and fence posts stuck
deep inside the ground. At night, your hands
                              like spiders crawl
back to their places. Quickly, love deteriorates to the empty insides
of my sneakers, *You're not going anywhere.*
                              How come, darling,
there isn't a police force?
                    That's because, baby, there aren't any rules.
Walnuts churn under car wheels and bruise their yellow hulls.
Marble without is
              marble-colored. The bruising doesn't mean
my heart is made of stone. Fall slides
                              into winter like tires on the drive.
The ground we tread gets hard, then harder. From an evergreen,
birds seed the sky. Yesterday, you said to me,
                              Birds don't get pregnant.
That's true. Birds can also fly. Described
                              in pictures, described
in words—*achingly beautiful*—more tender than we
ever could have imagined.

5:07 p.m. ——

Leaves curled like the crumpled fists of infants.
Snow crowns a bird's nest, a cupcake,
or a baked and slit sweet potato.

And you say I am sad,
that I have an icy sadness.
I frown. I'm not sad
to fixate on the light fixture.
I can see it through the curtainless window.

Scatter Plot

I would never compare men to God, but let me start
by saying—names or not—they all respond, or don't respond, to *you.*

The vacuum sucks a desert from the carpet—*varoom, room.* You enter
and say words to me, words I do not hear until you tear the cord-head out,

"—nothing," you say, "happens in a vacuum." An argument
proceeds from here, and you tell me to go to hell. I think I would like hell—

Hell, at least, is just,
                              its pain intelligible—unlike this world so full
of double standards and double talk and the double question,

So this is or is not about my faithlessness?

I thought we'd live
                              happily ever after—*ha, ha, ha.* I like to laugh,
an art that's empty and not tragic. Now Monday, on the radio, I say:

Bombs kill civilians in Kabul, a parade moves down South 4th Street.
Of course I would never compare the two, all events are separate, discrete.

But they happen simultaneously. And from behind a sound-proof pane,
my boss gives me two thumbs up. Anything is
                                                            better than dead air.

The only constellation I can recognize, Orion's Belt, lowers in the sky.
Nothing surprises me.
                              Art has not taught me to be ethical, but

the form of this feels wrong, wrong,

wrong. We weren't meant to be just
bright points in space and time.

There were supposed to be cords, strings connecting us, if only
in thought. And the cords were supposed to mean something to you

as well. I care for nothing
in your absence.

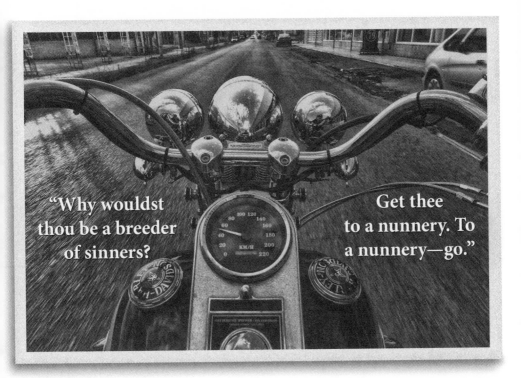

Dear Earnest,

The front of a motorcycle reminds me of my reproductive system—
handle bars the fallopian tubes, mirrors ovaries, headlight uterus,
and front wheel vagina.

Working in the barn, I fit my sweaty fingers in a glove,
and remember you at your cruelest,
"Get thee to a nunnery. To a nunnery—go."

I fit my other hand in the other glove and wriggle
thumb to pinky.
In the air in front of me, a little wave—

Say *bon voyage*.

I am searching for the objective,
I mean the objective correlative,
for the loss of a child that was not

a child—and it doesn't exist.

But E, I still can't help but feel
I have something to say about the sonnet form.

My heart is in two pieces.

Bird's-Eye View

EXT. THE STREET

Earnest thinks shrimp do not have legs
  and I am holding folders with kittens on them. "I'm a poet,"
  I say, "I like poetry."

INT. A MOVING VEHICLE

His lunch in a paper bag,
  his lunch on the floor beside his feet,
  the apple on top of the peanut butter sandwich,
  the sandwich being crushed—see how funny it is? That sandwich is
  absolutely crushed.
This is an experiment: a pair of cross-tracked lovers.
The shingles on the houses glisten in rain or shine.
On the street, people furl and unfurl their umbrellas.
It is raining, and as it rains, the raindrops turn round the wheels of trucks
  and rise as mist.
I'm dabbling in desolation, I'm dabbling in debilitation.
A pair of cross-tracked lovers—and honestly—
  who comes up with this?
He is going to stick his hand down my shirt when I see the plastic trash bag
  in the road in front of us, flapping in the wind and rain, a bruised eyelid,
  and have to swerve.
I have been driving for a long time and haven't hit anyone yet, but, *baby—
  that's dangerous.*
I'm having trouble feeling anything, and he says, "You don't seem to feel
  pain, Eleanor.
You're numb and cold like some sort of lower, lower form of life."

The shadows from the dumpsters fan out and slide down the hillside,
      and the little pebbles that make up the hillside stay
      in their places—remain motionless—miles and miles
      of hearts of stone.
The tarantulas on the roadway and all the little animals in the forest
      freeze in the headlights—
      turn to stone.
I drive over the shadows on the highway.
I'm terrible—don't forget that—I'm evil and was born it,
      but, Earnest, you do not think
      shrimp have legs.
This is an experiment
      to see if I can be kind—to see if I can lie—
      and I like words too much. I know all women do,
      but I'm not going to lie. I am a lower, lower form of life.

EXT. RESORT PARKING LOT

The shingles on the cabins glisten in rain or shine.
This is the parking lot. This is our stop. And I get out
      to have a cigarette. One car pulls from its parking spot
      in the fading light; the car in front eclipses one headlight.
It seems like an accident that we are here together. Perhaps it is
      an accident that we are here at all. Already, men are trying to help.
I know I won't be able to carry anything—
      not my suitcase, not my remembered pain, not even this thought.
I will be given a key. I will walk to a threshold that I will cross,
      then I'll be naked. They call this vacation.

They call it recreation. I will not remember what
        the weather was, but before I give it up,
I point my umbrella outward and to the side and collapse
        a single tooth. The silver ribs shut the black skin quickly. Like an eye.

I:58 p.m. ——

The hand of God is about to come down and rip the tops off houses,
then it is not.

Would you descend for the sandwiches? I stop

trying to write the upstairs window, its pane
too transparent to describe.

Calm Down

The sun bounces on the floor of the horizon, and I still feel this,
      the first ounce of haught I have ever felt, collecting
                        behind my jaw. Help.
      Earnest is turning into a lizard
sunning himself by the pool. He sticks a Dorito in his mouth,
      and it makes a crunching sound. The bag
                a net of light, creases, shines
and crinkles. He broke my nose—

When I say *I'm tortured,* why is this not funny? When I say,
I've been tortured, he tortured me, clearly I don't mean it—
                Why is this not funny?

Calm down, Eleanor. I'm sad and sadness only breeds more
      sadness, like sandwiches cut into pieces, cut
                into triangular pieces.
      The sunlight descending on the sweaty tropics,
the sun trying to look
      demure.

His hand came crashing down on me like a piece of ceiling and broke
the wave, dammed for a moment, the stream of light and my nose
              broken. Look—
more demure.

      The pool is only a carpet of water
           threaded with waves of light.

The red triangles make a crunch. I tell the joke until
    it is funny. The punch line: *You bitch,*

                    you've ruined my life.

My nose is still broken. The soda bottles in the rack—
Soda bottles. White caps.

II:03 a.m. ——

A tree branch smacks the white wood fence, like a hand.
Leaves poke through holes shaped like diamonds,
for a moment, flat as paddles, then retreat—
behind the fence, between the leaves,
beach.

Your eyes are apple seeds.

Snap a picture?

You apologize.
We smile, we take a photograph. We're fine.

I choose not to focus anymore.

What You Are Eating as Metaphor for What You Want Right Now

You turn the brownie into two brownies
by cutting it in two.
You didn't think a boy could break your daughter's heart, especially not that boy,
but there it is.

By cutting it in two
he broke your daughter's heart.
There it is—in two pieces.
You think of her as you look at the ocean.

He broke my heart, Mom.
Do you ever get bored of hearing it?
*We were sitting on a park bench looking out at the water, and we thought
    of you—*
crying an ocean—

———

Do you ever get bored of hearing it? The crickets in the park
make their cricket sounds—
crying an ocean—you know what crickets sound like. They sound nice
their entire bodies vibrating.

The crickets make their cricket sounds.
You hear through the phone the one sound you never wanted to hear—and it is
    creaking.
You know what crickets sound like—nice.
You look down as the green slats run through your thighs.

The one sound you never wanted to hear—and it's breaking.
You cut the brownie in two.
I stare down at the green running through my thighs.
I didn't think a boy could break my heart, but there it is—

two pieces.

Wedding Planning

I begin to dread the surf and turf. I cross
then double cross another friend off of the list. Now this,
"The jaws of leopard seals and grizzly bears are similar,
except the leopard seals' are twice as big. They're also more intelligent."
God knows my mother likes to tell me things
I do not want to know in restaurants.
"This scientist, she studied icebergs in Antarctica.
She watched them drift and scour the sea floor,
and the ensuant loss of life and habitat—"
This story I know cold and could deglove.

Snow settled round the research base, like a halo.
The ancient face, the surface, of the bay
under a layer of jostling, floating crags—"brash ice."

Birds flew in fists into the teeth of sky.
Whether she believed in God or anything below us,
wind furred the shallows and she snorkeled out.

"The leopard seal attacked from underneath,
and so she must have seen the open jaws, the teeth. She screamed,
was dragged, her dive computer says, to a depth of 230 feet."

I cross another friend off of my list.
Punishment should be immediate,
but accident cannot be reckoned with.
This is the myth inside decorum—
and what I've ordered never does arrive.

You Marry a Man

You marry a man and you think his blood is red.
Turns out it's not, it's purple.

This doesn't matter, is not why you married him,
but you did—you thought his blood was red.

And he has never read Shakespeare, knows nothing
of the quality of mercy, but he reminds you every day
that you are not Shakespeare.

You know you're not Shakespeare, Eleanor, he says.

He says this to you as you peel and eat a doleful Dole banana.

That is fine, too. When you habitate with someone—

He is saying now that "habitate" is not a word [in the dictionary], and maybe not in the dictionary, but I heard it on a nature program. *Who died and made you police of the English language?*—

You have to put up with a few statements of the obvious. Example: *What are you doing?* —Obvious. *What do you think you are doing?* —Should be obviously inferable.

What are you reading? —This is what they make book covers for.

But it could be worse, he could be saying things that are untrue, he could be saying things that are wrong.

I invite you, my darling, to consider the difference between untrue and wrong. I feel you often avoid saying things that are untrue by stating the obvious. I feel you often say things that are wrong.

And then there are things there are two ways of looking at: the banana on the counter. With its ends pointed up it looks happy, looks, in fact, like a smile.

But with its ends pointed down it looks doleful again.

Or maybe it is just that we both have different definitions.

I thought "I do" was self-explanatory. You didn't.

We have different definitions of pain. What I think hurts and what you think hurts me, are very different. And it is not just the things you think, but the things you don't think that hurt me as well.

I bleed. *Don't you see?* This is not about whose blood is redder—You're an alien!—and I forgive you even that, but I bleed. The point is I bleed.

And then he says, "I have the dictionary on my lap."

You don't own the dictionary, baby. *We both own it.* The speech that ends all conversation. There is nothing to be said to heal this. I have the dictionary in my lap.

Look at the words betraying their meanings (betray as in desert in time of need). Look at the words betraying their meanings (betray as in reveal). Look at the words—

Sonnet: Boston Proper

In Providence, my boss said, "Hesitation kills."
Was true then, is true now. The radio replayed,
We want a lady in the street, a freak in bed.
The spaces in between I don't know how to fill.

Three times I've ridden in a horse-drawn carriage like
a character from Austen's *Pride and Prejudice*,
as towers built by Puritans' offspring—tactless—
cast phallic shadows over cobble streets—oblique
junctions, chevrons of stone—outdone, but not outclassed.

The first, you asked why I loved you. I did not know,
I did not know what I should say. This is my fate.
The horse hooves kissed the street. One horse, one of a pair,
broke to canter—a three-beat, not a two-beat, gait—
and each beat registered on your face like a blow.

The steel beams rigid, towers elastic in air.

3:39 p.m. ——

Sites I will see every day for the rest of my life, I imagine:
FIRST BAPTIST   MAUI TANS   CATFISH. They're renting
space.

I want a new form of recreation. So I put my hands in gloves
and meet my golf instructor in the clubhouse—
a pot with greenery and the words   CHARGER FIELD.
The plants, the plants on the window ledge, the plants on the links,
the only living things not lying down in the heat,
which is punishing. A dimpled shock of white,
the cotton tumbles, pools   over in a ditch.
There are worse things than cheating.
Losing is one.

The Ballad of Eleanor and Earnest

Part I—Predestination

From their hometown of Paris, Tennessee, the adulteress and her lover embark on a road trip to New Orleans. Her lover drives and speaks.

"The Puritans got a bad rep
for being humorless,"
Earnest says on a car trip,
"but they had some good ideas.

Life is like *Terminator 2:
Judgment Day*, like this trip—
pre-scripted, as 'To be, or not . . . '
the question is bullshit.

You can't be whatever you want,
or do whatever you want.
You can't even say what you want,
not without consequence."

Eleanor looks out the window
the pane of which reminds—
in her dreams, as a child, transparent dragons
were circling, circling always,

One image leads to another in the adulteress' mind.

animating the landscape with their transparent scales,
and she was terrified.
She always wanted to cry, cry out—
"Fire! Fire! Fire!"—
a moment too soon, the only time she could
do anyone any good.

Our heroine! Yelling "Fire!" Fire indeed!

What naïve and childish pluck!
When, ultimately, it comes down to
a simple game of luck—
tails you're saved, but heads you burn.

Part II—The Mirror Up To

From the passenger seat, the
adulteress recounts her
weekend with her husband.

Eleanor knows fate is fate,
but she wants still to change
the subject. "With coworkers, we spent
our Sunday at The Chain

nominating and electing
each other. Rob won
'I Like to Watch Movies Where Things Blowup,'
a category I would have won

if there was any justice in the world.
I won 'Best Pickup' for
Are you from Tennessee?
Because you're the only ten I see."—"You whore!"

(Earnest says). As if on cue,
they laugh and laugh and laugh.
Although it wasn't (objectively) that funny,
her winning line outclassed

the pickup *I wish I was a mirror*
so I could see myself . . .
The losing line was more poetic

I'm the poet. I can't help but
insert myself into the poem.

and (often) more true. I do.
I wish I was a mirror—a mirror—
so I could see myself.

Part III—Literal Interpretation

As the lovers near the West
Tennessee State Penitentiary,
the adulteress contemplates
the signage.

The signs along the road, she feels,
loom large and numerous—
FOR SALE, one reads, FOR SALE, FOR SALE!
PECANS (with a phone number).

The signs are hard to comprehend—

Signage is largely useless.

ANTIOCH   MISSIONARY   BAPTIST.

The prison she mistakes for a castle
(for the seventh time), and cries.
"You're acting crazy," Earnest says.
He doesn't spell out why.

I agree. I think capital
punishment is wrong, but
whether or not God agrees is
another question.

CAPITAL PUN. IS   ALWAYS,   ALWAYS
WRONG. Earnest says,
"You have to tell me what you want." Like the Bible,
she fears the words once said

that cannot be and cannot be
unsaid. "You just have to."
And like the Bible, she wonders if
this is literally true.
"I want," she says, "to leave him and
I want to live with you."

5:37 p.m. ——

The Washington Monument in miniature
sticks out of the trees   by BUTLER SNOW,
fake, but real. You'll think this poem is about sex—
fucking. You don't think much   of me.
I know all about fucking, but this is not
Gluckstadt, MS—the BUSINESS PARK green sign,
and the heat that seemed
not inside or outside, but everywhere,
an atmosphere. *The Beautiful Ms., the Beautiful Ms.*
You're so hot, you said.

If Tony Hoagland Was Right

Poetry should talk to God, but herein lies
a quandary: If God knows everything,

then what is there to say? We need
intermediaries? Perhaps my teacher

was right again, and poetry should also
tell a story. In the parking lot of Dairy Queen,

Eleanor and Earnest smoke and rest
their cups of soft-serve ice cream

on the roof of her husband's Ram pickup.
The ice cream looks like horns, but sweats

like flesh. The truck is hot and numb, she thinks,
mechanical, a beautiful machine, means

nothing. Eleanor is naïve, not dumb.
Earnest watches TV through an adjacent sports bar

window. A game, played in a dome—
soccer, the World Cup, I think—

and on the techni-green, a player
writhes and writhes

with pain he does not feel.
I've faked it, and I can tell you—

that ain't real. Dear God,
you know how to keep a secret.

I suppose I can tell you now
I never read *The Faerie Queene,* and I don't believe

in allegory. Life has its start and stop
and kicks, perhaps, but

play is not continuous. It's also useless
to tell you it's not fair. Now my teacher

is dead. Cancer. Horrible suffering
and I invented Eleanor and Earnest

for some forgotten reason. They're both
so lurid and despicable. All I know is

I am resisting the temptation
to tell you this is wrong—but, yes,

yes, yes, yes, O, God, yes—
I perform and am dishonest.

Pantoum for Earnest

Dear Earnest, I have been thinking for a long time about us,
        and sometimes Donald Trump.
Sometimes I am like Donald Trump,
        and sometimes you are like Donald Trump,
            and sometimes Donald Trump is like us—
We cannot say what we mean.
        And sometimes, Walt Whitman, you are like Donald Trump—
        you contradict yourself.

We cannot say what we mean.
        Donald Trump says, *History is watching us.* So history sees
        you contradict yourself.
Last winter, the snow, this spring, the grass blades,
        and Donald Trump says, *History is watching us now.*
        I don't understand history. I never did.
This spring, the grass blades in their uniform
        shades of green—repeat, repeat, repeat.

I don't understand history. I never did. But history is
        just motion in a larger field, like TV,
        repeats, repeats, repeats.

I have been thinking for a long time, dear Earnest,
        we are motion, like TV.
        I am in earnest, Earnest! And I am like Donald Trump—

My words don't mean a thing.

In history class, the professor says,
  "We tend to idealize the past."

Dear E,

Last winter, the snow in sheets of laundered white,
this spring, the grass blades kissed and cuddled in their bed
with the slightest breeze

and I led horses named for weather—Misty, Hurricane, and Twister—
to their paddocks, fences stitched on the hillside, in Rhode Island,
which, you know, is not an island.

The horses nuzzled at my shoulders
with their drumming, peach-skin noses. Once they were free,
their naked crests ran through the meadow
then dropped to eat.

I don't understand history, I never did. But history is
just motion in a summer field.

It's been a long time, Earnest. Please forgive
the public nature of this postcard.

I only think of you.

I2:52 p.m. ——

Look at my dress
take the shape of my lap—

Sometimes you have to change
the subject. But the laundry basket
is an innocent thing.

Don't drag it into this.

On Being and Dry-Cleaning: A Series of Steps

Call me Eleanor. Or call me Earnest. This stoic dry-cleaning machine is the Galaxy.

Names are often deceiving.

Dry-cleaning is, in fact, a wet business, but is waterless—is, most basically, a chemical process by which stains are brought to the surface of fabrics to be skimmed off using steam. Most cleaners use a liquid solvent called perchloroethylene, or perc. There are three main advantages to dry-cleaning.

First: Some fabrics, such as silk, shrink or warp when submerged in water, but do not lose their form in perc.

Next: Oil is not soluble in water but will dissolve in perc, making dry-cleaning especially effective at removing food stains.

Think businessman. Think appetite. Now think of his tie.

What is this but a glorified bib? And what can water do?

Finally: My hands do not get dirty.

The Galaxy looks like a front-loading washing machine, only bigger, and operates like a combination washer and dryer.

Once the circular hatch is shut, a drum fills with solvent, agitates, drains, spins, and finally dries.

The clothes are then removed from the belly, spot-treated with a steam-pen, pressed, and bagged. But these steps do not interest me.

I reason, because the clothes are already clean.

I claw through libraries and drive through states; I quote Melville to say *I am in earnest; and I will try*; and I grow cold, and pale, and distant.

I am told I lack

yearning.

This is true.

To feel the *text* in textile, I must do with these visible hands.

Some fabrics cannot be dry-cleaned.

Before the invention of rubber there were, of course, no rubber clothes.

At first, rubber was made from trees, *Hevea brasiliensis*, the South American rubber tree. Today, latex is the raw material from which most rubber is made and for this reason condoms are called rubbers and defined as such in the dictionary: "**rubber 3 d :** CONDOM."

Latex is milky and (usually) white, excreted by various seed plants, including milkweed, spurge, and poppy, but latex can also be made synthetically, like prose

and poetry.

Prose protects and lyric ornaments, but, like rubber clothing, they are only shadows of the human form. Towards the end of the day, one shrinks and the other stretches, and discomfits the body beneath.

I have suffered long enough to understand I live

somewhere along Plato's Divided Line, and I don't live in Episteme.

Synthetic latex is an emulsion of synthetic rubber or plastic in water (an emulsion is the mixture of one liquid in another, immiscible liquid—which seems impossible, but happens every day, as in fat in milk).

So latex is a colloid, a substance which is, in fact, two distinct substances—one dispersed throughout the other. Or, the less precise definition, "**col • loid 2 b :** a colloid together with the medium in which it is dispersed <smoke is a ~>."

Few things are pure, thus many things are colloids.

Smoke is a colloid, as is love.

Perhaps the soul is—

I can think of others, but latex is the important one.

Before the invention of rubber clothing there were, of course, no rubber fetishists.

In most rubber apparel rubber fibers are at the core of the yarn and cotton fibers are wrapped around them.

Remember when Conrad wrote in *Heart of Darkness* that it was not the core or kernel Marlow was concerned with, but everything outside, in the surrounding haze? This is not that yarn.

This yarn is elastic, like a second skin, ideal for form-fitting clothing.

Rubber is also used to coat fabrics, most commonly rain-gear and drapes. Rubber is flexible, strong, and nonabsorbent, but also hot

and uncomfortable. Cotton breathes. Rubber does not.

Rubber is damaged by sunlight, oil, and sweat. And rubber cannot be dry-cleaned: components mixed with rubber dissolve during dry-cleaning and stain adjacent fabric; heat drying makes rubber hard and brittle; and steam finishing causes rubber fabric to pucker, blister, peel, and stick

like a synthetic sore.

There have, of course, been leather fetishists for a long, long time.

I used to own a lot of leather and used it all the time—all serious horseback riders do. I owned leather boots and breeches with suede knee patches; and I owned leather tack—a saddle, girth, bridle, breastplate, martingale, and a set of yoke reins. I went through a pair of leather boots a year. I often wore a hole straight through the side, at my calf. This hole would appear right as the stitching above my toes gave out. The last time I saw my saddle it had mold growing on it, like the grass already pushing up through someone's ribs.

I gave up a form of recreation

and material things, things I loved unambiguously—loved

in black and white—to make a living. I wound up cleaning

strangers' clothing.

And leather, like rubber, is a pain in the ass to clean.

The International Fabricare Institute begins its bulletin on leather: "Leather is nature's non-woven fabric." To make leather, the skin from animals is stripped, cured, and rolled around in drums.

Roll, like an 18-wheeler—

that ho fine, but this ho a killer.

The radio is always on and, as I work, I aspire to the quality of song.

The dictionary defines hide as "the skin of an animal whether raw or dressed—used esp. of large heavy skins," or "the life or physical well-being of a person <betrayed his friend to save his own ~>." There is one other definition of hide.

All hides have three layers.

The first layer holds the hair follicles. Every animal has a unique hair pattern—like snowflakes. The wool is left intact in many sheepskin garments to make a warm, inner lining. You are not cold, but hot—hot blooded. You notice, after all, a perfect, female form.

The bottom layer of a hide, then, is the flesh. The flesh is the outer surface of a traditional sheepskin garment. We just cut the sheep open and turn it inside out.

The Fabricare Institute again says that the "general adage" is, "The harder the life of the animal the better quality of the skin." If this is hard for you to read, then maybe you shouldn't wear leather. If not, fine. You look nice, sexy even.

Till you percolate. Make it work,

with your wet t-shirt—

Bitch, you gotta shake it till your calf muscles hurt.

If the animal was cut, however, during life and healed, even if it was just bitten by an insect, the healed skin will be thicker, and will absorb dyes and oils differently than the rest of the hide.

"Bleeding" refers to dyes loosened during washing—like the red trim that turns your sock pink, or the red shirt that pinks your underwear. Bleeding is not usually a problem with leather, but leather dye will often partially dissolve or wear away during cleaning or drying.

Cleaning may also reduce the oil content of leather. A hide drained of oil will appear drained of color, and oiling after cleaning will darken the hide again.

Thus scar tissue is a natural defect that may become more apparent upon cleaning.

Like song, work is rhythmic,

repetitive, but work strips us of things to sing

concerning.

Roll, like an 18-wheeler—that ho fine,

but this ho kill her.

A cowhide is large enough to make a garment with no seams, but is too thick, so is split, sometimes into three, sometimes into five sheets.

When the skin is split, veins are brought closer to the surface and sometimes split as well. Like scar tissue, vein channels absorb dye and oil differently and can become more prominent after cleaning. Veins will appear as lighter cobwebs above a darker mass. Or, the vein can fall out during cleaning

leaving an empty canal

that looks like a groove from a knife. Rock bottom is not

empty, but peopled, trafficked—I think that is what surprised me the most. Cars rush through their lanes like blood cells, their lights red and white in the damp darkness, following a white truck (like a whale), the canvas sides of the truck expanding and contracting, expanding and contracting. The last living, breathing, hot-blooded mammal is hounded.

And you're laughing. You think this is silly. "Ha, ha, ha—Moby *Dick*." This is not, not silly.

She's leakin'—she's soaking wet. She's leakin'—soaking wet.

I want to be with you and keep you warm. A perfect pair of chaps.

I2:I5 p.m. ——

My breasts in a bathing suit, two sails caught by a small wind—

there is spittle on my chest because I have leaned over and drooled.

But I do, I do know what you said. For the thousandth time—

you said that time, like light, is both particulate and liquid.

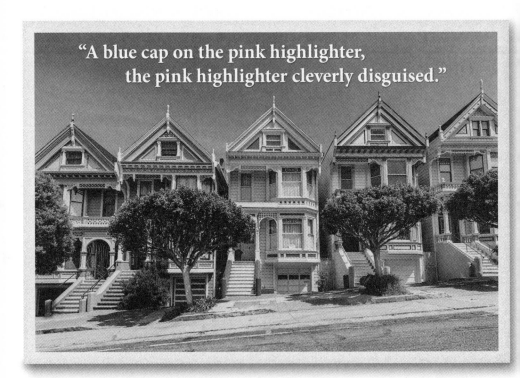

"A blue cap on the pink highlighter,
the pink highlighter cleverly disguised."

Dear Earnest, I wonder if our child would have been male or cursed.

The rows and rows of houses, different colors at different layers, like cake,
and two tree trunks that end
in veiny leaves and seeds, like two fresh-cut hay bales side by side
and raised in air.
                    O to be an angel looking down
or God in Infinite and Sexless Wisdom, and not have
to look out
                    or to look up.
                                        Sex: the sum
of characteristics involved in reproduction
that distinguish males and females.

I know. I thought it would be different, too.

If you wanted to know what sex was,
Earnest, I could have told you. I could have saved us both.

In the Cartoon Version of Your Life,
Birds Sing in English

Every day men flay the inside

of the building. *Of course*
they aren't all men, that would be illegal—We aren't being
literal.

They rise up centrally through the elevators and
fan out, each man a knot,

tied by a black line of energy
to a distant purpose. Without that energy

we would fall
through the world that so deeply absorbs us.

The building is gray,
the men are pink. They flit inside the building, like fish
inside a coral reef.

The building has an inner beauty
the two-dimensional ocean has

never seen, never will.
We are not drowning.

All night the sun sets and pinks
the outside of the building, too.

Pink is a pretty hue.

On Valentine's Day, G hands L a card sewn with paper hearts.
G is trembling, like a daisy, and as he does
the hearts shake, *Dearest,*

This is very disturbing.

Today,

in a gray classroom—*excuse me*—gray *conference* room,
covered by a gray ceiling, we learn the favoritism

G lavishes

on the woman he is sleeping with

is not unlawful.

The color of the ceiling illuminated by tough, fluorescing
light, filters down

through our airways, through

our breathing.

I worry for the deer in the woods, worry
because they are so tame. They fear no men. They chomp
the grass so naïvely, the sound of their teeth going, like
jackhammers in their heads.

Oh, Dearie! Oh dearie,

dearie, dearie, dearie, dearie. Dear Bambi—blank stares—
Oh, Bambi! *You don't know who Bambi is.*

We have lost our sense of place

again. It was fun while it lasted.

NOTES

"Earnest Postcard": *Why wouldst thou be a breeder of sinners? . . . Get thee to a nunnery. . . . To a nunnery, go,* is some of what Hamlet says to Ophelia in 3.1. The "objective correlative" is T. S. Eliot's coinage from "Hamlet and His Problems."

"Wedding Planning": On July 22, 2003, Kirsty Brown, a marine biologist, was snorkeling off the coast of Antarctica when she was dragged underwater and drowned by a leopard seal. She was 28. Hers is the first documented human death caused by a leopard seal and is believed to be the first of its kind.

"You Marry a Man": *The quality of mercy* is from *The Merchant of Venice.* The definitions of *betray* are adapted from *Merriam-Webster's Collegiate Dictionary: Tenth Edition.*

"Sonnet: Boston Proper": *We want a lady in the street, but a freak in the bed* is a line from Ludacris' feature on "Yeah!"

"The Ballad of Eleanor and Earnest": *To be, or not* is from Hamlet's soliloquy in 3.1. *The mirror up to [nature]* is from Hamlet's instructions to the actors in 3.2.

"Pantoum for Earnest": In his speech accepting the Republican presidential nomination on July 21, 2016, Donald Trump said, *History is watching us now. . . . History is watching.*

"On Being and Dry-Cleaning": The definitions of *rubber, colloid,* and *hide* are from *Merriam-Webster.* Plato describes the Divided Line in *The Republic,* book VI. *Moby Dick* and a bulletin on leather care from *Fabricare: The Magazine of the International Fabricare Institute* are sampled as are lyrics from "Salt Shaker" by the Ying Yang Twins.

"Earnest Postcard": The definition of *sex* is from *Merriam-Webster.*

Many thanks to the magazines where the following poems (or earlier versions) first appeared:

American Poetry Review: "The Heart Is Not a Synonym for the Chest" and "Scatter Plot"; *Barrow Street*: "Pantoum for Earnest"; *Boudin: The Online Home of the McNeese Review*: [Earnest Postcard], "Bird's-Eye View," and [Earnest Postcard]; *Copper Nickel*: "What You Are Eating as Metaphor for What You Want Right Now" and "Wedding Planning"; *FIELD*: "One Thousand Words on Regret"; *JERRY*: "Historically, We Haven't Taken Any Prisoners" and "In the Cartoon Version of Your Life, Birds Sing in English"; *Mudfish*: "You Marry a Man"; *New American Writing*: "Sonnet: Boston Proper"; *Salt Hill Journal*: "If Tony Hoagland Was Right"; *Tin House*: [Earnest Postcard]; *Waxwing*: "On Being and Dry-Cleaning: A Series of Steps"; *Willow Springs*: "Calm Down."

Thanks

To Tanya Grae. I doubted, you didn't. I don't know how to thank you, *but thank you*. You taught me so much by example and you helped shape this book.

To Dorsey Craft and Alexa Doran. I am incredibly grateful for your poetry, your input, and your friendship. Also, you listened to so many of my strange and weird stories. Most of them were too long, but thank you for saying they weren't.

To my teachers (in the order I met them): Lynn Brown, Kris Thomson, D. A. Powell, Peter Richards, Jorie Graham, Peter Sacks, Lauren Brozovich, Bret Anthony Johnston, Kevin Prufer, Roberto Tejada, Sally Connolly, Nick Flynn, Tony Hoagland, Martha Serpas, Erin Belieu, Andrew Epstein, Barbara Hamby, and James Kimbrell.

To James Kimbrell's 2018 manuscript workshop: Marianne Chan, Dorsey Craft, William Fargason, Tanya Grae, Jessie King, Paige Lewis, Brandi Nicole Martin, and Dustin Pearson.

To the many inspiring and supportive writers and friends I met at Florida State University, the University of Houston, and Harvard University.

To the people I lived with while I wrote these poems: Danielle McCullough, Kristen Lozada Morgan, Natalie Lawson, Jennie Laree Tobler-Gaston, and Katelyn Stark.

To my Tallahassee tennis partners (also in the order I met them): Lee Patterson, Zach Gerberick, Jon Mundell, Clancy McGilligan, Farrah Hersh, Kelsey Mrjoian, and Jamous McQueen. I know it's just a game, but tennis got me through some dire times.

To the artists whose images I used for the "Earnest Postcards." Special thanks to Chuck Haney. Your image came first and helped me choose the rest.

To the editors and staff at the University of Pittsburgh Press, especially Ed Ochester and Alex Wolfe.

To many more wonderful people, experiences, and texts than I can name here. Poets are sponges, and I am deeply indebted to you all.

To my parents. I know you don't enjoy my poetry. Thank you for encouraging me anyway. I love you.

To my brother. I love you, too.

And, finally, to Cascade. You understood. I miss you.